WHAT TO REMEMBER
TO BE HAPPY

What To Remember To Be Happy

*A Spiritual Way of Life
for Your First Fourteen Years or So*

By Da Free John

THE DAWN HORSE PRESS
CLEARLAKE, CALIFORNIA

First edition published February 1978
Second edition, May 1979
Third edition, February 1982
Reprinted October 1984

Printed in the United States of America

International Standard Book Number 0-913922-36-6

Produced by The Johannine Daist Communion in cooperation with The Dawn Horse Press

Have you heard this

is an apple?

Have you been told this

is a tree?

Do you think this

is the moon?

and this

the sun?

Have you told someone this

is a little girl

and this

is a little boy?

Well. But you and I can be very truthful to each other. And it seems to me that no matter what we name

this

or this

or this

or this

or this

or this

we still do not know what they **are**. Truly, you and I don't know what a single thing **is**. Do you know what I am? See. And I don't know what you are either. It is a Mystery. Doesn't it make you feel good to feel it?

Did you ever ask somebody where

this

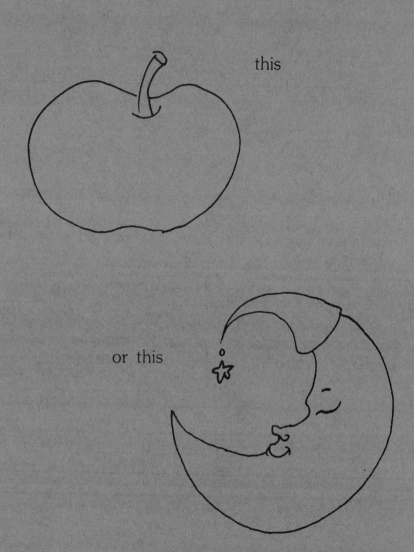

or this

or this

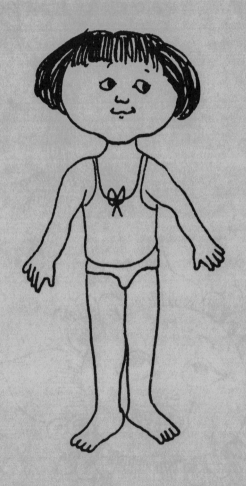

came from,

or how this

or this

or this

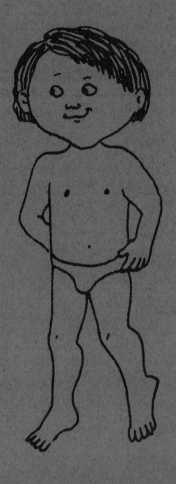

came to be? Some say, "I don't know" and saying this makes them feel they are being very honest and truthful. Others say something such as "God made it" or "It comes from God." And such people are also being very honest and truthful when they say this.

How can they both be telling the truth? Well, because they are both telling you the same thing in different ways. You see, **nobody,** not Mom, or Dad, or Grandmother, or Grandfather, or big Sister, or big Brother, or teachers, or doctors, or soldiers, or reverends, or athletes, or lawyers, or TV stars, or any people who are working, or any people who are playing, not even the President, not even a King or a Queen, not even people who love each other know what a single thing **is.** It is a great and wonderful Mystery to all of us that anything is, or that we are. And whether somebody says "I don't know how anything came to be" or "God made everything" they are simply pointing to the feeling of the Mystery, of how everything is but nobody knows what it really is or how it came to be.

As long as we go on feeling this Mystery, we feel free and full and happy, and we feel and act free and full and happy to others. This is the secret of being happy from the time you are small until the time you are old.

Everybody, even all the animals, goes on living for a while, and then the part of them we see and touch and talk to every day when we wake up goes to sleep in the feeling of the Mystery. This happens to everybody. And everybody has to live every day without being afraid to go to sleep. This can be difficult, even when you are small. Because, especially people sometimes forget the Mystery and get unhappy and try to make others feel unhappy by making them know or think things that make them afraid and forget the Mystery.

So the way to keep on being happy every day until you go to sleep is to remember the Mystery. Just keep on remembering that you, with everybody else, do not know what a single thing is,

not even a

Just remember this, or remember God, which is the same thing. Keep on remembering God or the Mystery and you will feel happy and act happy to others, and so you will keep on loving and helping others so the world won't get all afraid and stupid and unable to sleep or play or work.

If you do this all the time, you will have lots of amazing and wonderful experiences until you go back to sleep. And if you remember the Mystery even when you are going to sleep, then you will go to sleep all happy in the Mystery. And you will always wake up in the Mystery too. And all your dreams will be about the Mystery until you wake up again.

Remembering the Mystery is a way of being everything you always already are. When you sleep you are something different than when you wake up. And when you dream you are different too. The way you seem to be when you wake up is only one of the ways you are.

Some day, everybody has what they look like go to sleep and not wake up. Then they forget that part, and they go on to someplace else and look different. Nobody knows what they will look like after what they look like now goes to sleep forever. When you go to sleep at night you forget what you looked like all day. And when somebody "dies," or lets the body go to sleep for the last time, they forget what they looked like when they were alive and awake. It is a Mystery, like going to sleep, or dreaming, or waking up.

So, whether we look like   or

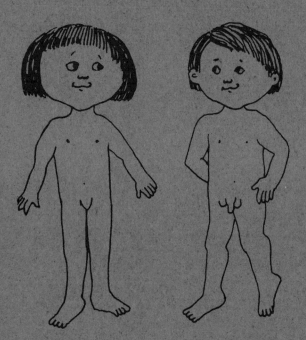

we are not only the way we look.

Well. There are three good things to remember lots of times every day if we are going to stay happy and keep on loving and not be afraid. They are three ways of remembering the Mystery, or staying the way we really are before we start to name things and think and know about anything. Before we name or think or know, we already **are** and we already **feel.**

The first thing to remember a lot when you are awake is to **feel** the Mystery. **Feel** God. Feel that you don't know what a single thing **is**. You may know the name of something or someone. You may know about all kinds of somethings and someones. But you do not and you cannot know what anything or anyone **is**. Nobody does, and nobody can. It is important to remember and feel this a lot. When you do this you feel quiet and you forget all the names, and you forget to be afraid, and you stop thinking, and you only feel good, and true, and full of love, and radiating.

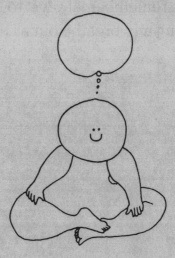

And when you feel the Mystery real strong you can tell that you even breathe the Mystery. When people feel the Mystery real strong and breathe it they say things like "God is Spirit" because Spirit is just a name for what we feel about our breath. When people say things like this they are only feeling very happy. They don't know anything more than before about God. They are just Wondering, how the Mystery even goes all through them and doesn't have any shape or face or up or down or inside or outside.

Well. When you remember to feel the Mystery real strong, then you can also remember to breathe the Mystery. The Mystery is good feeling full of light and love, isn't it? So when you breathe the Mystery, remember always to breathe in all the good feeling and breathe out all the bad feeling.

Breathe in all the happy feeling about the Mystery, and breathe out all the unhappy feelings you might be thinking about, like being afraid, or angry, or selfish, or mean, or just unhappy. Stand up and feel to yourself "Breathe in the good stuff—Breathe out the bad stuff" again and again.

It is good to do this every now and then every day. It is a way to get to remember the Mystery stronger and stronger, and I'll bet you start to feel so good after a while that it seems like you aren't remembering and breathing the Mystery anymore but the Mystery is remembering and breathing you!

What a Wonderful Mystery the Mystery is.

The second thing to remember a lot every day is that you are always more than what you look like. The part that is the way you look is only you while you are awake and alive. But the rest of you goes on while you sleep and dream, and after the body "dies" or goes to sleep for good, the rest of you goes on in the Mystery. The way to remember this is to see and feel **everything** that is yourself all the time. The body part, the way you look when you are awake, is only part of the way you are. You also feel and think when you are awake and when you dream, even though the body is forgotten. But even more than this is the way you can feel yourself to be in the Mystery.

It is a good idea, along with remembering to feel the Mystery all the time, to sit down every day for a little bit. Feel the Mystery real strong and breathe it until your breathing becomes real quiet and you are only feeling the Mystery really quiet and strong. Then close your eyes and put one of your fingers in each ear, so you can't hear any noises in the room or outside your face. Then listen inside. Listen up toward the top of your head with your eyes closed. Try it now, and then come back to reading again.

Well. Did you Hear? All the sounds inside your face? There is ringing and zinging and popping and fluting and wheezing and strumming and ocean roaring and booming and buzzing and all kinds of sounds like birds and crickets and music, and lots of quiet too.

Now put a finger over each eye, with your eyes closed and looking up inside toward the top of your head. Try it now, and then come back to reading again.

Did you See? There are lights and zigzags and lightning and stars and moving shiny spots and shivering shapes and all kinds of spaces and moons and suns and even places and all kinds of things to see, like in dreams, and really too.

It is good and fun and Mysterious to do this with your ears and eyes every day so you will remember to feel what you are that is more than what you look like. You are electrical and you are light and sound, whatever all of that may be. If people don't forget to feel this they stay happy and not afraid to love or to die, but they go on and on.

So far you have two things to remember a lot every day.

First, remember to feel the Mystery and even breathe it. Second, remember to feel you are more than you look like. (And a good way to do this is to sit and relax and feel the Mystery with your eyes and ears closed up at the same time, like when you are asleep.)

3.

The third thing it is good to remember every day is that **you** do the feeling and breathing and listening and looking and naming all the time. **You** aren't anything you know or feel or see or hear or look like or name or think. All these things just happen, and **you** get to watch or know or think them. **You** feel and see your own body or your inside sounds or lights or dreams or all the places that come up.

You think the names of

and

and

and

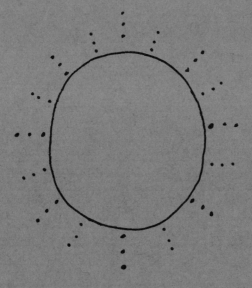

and   and

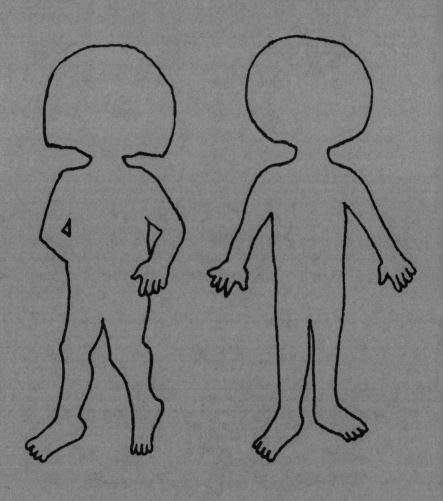

Y ou even think "I" and "me" and "mine." Well, what are you if you only watch all of these things?

You are the Mystery! Yes. You don't know what **you** are either! It is all the Mystery, and you yourself are the Mystery. It is all one Feeling.

If you will remember every day to feel the Mystery and if you will remember to feel that you are more than what you look like, and if you will remember to be the Mystery itself, then you will be happy every day. And all kinds of wonderful happenings will come up for you. You will feel happy and you will always help and love others, even those who are having trouble feeling happy and are even trying to make you forget the Mystery.

It is good to spend a lot of your time talking about the Mystery with others, instead of talking about unhappiness and things that happen when we forget to love. People who also feel the Mystery and love it are the best friends to have. Someday you may meet someone who has felt the Mystery really strong for a long time, so that person feels the Mystery all the time and is always happy. Such a person is the best person to learn from about happiness and life and love.

I hope you will remember to feel the Mystery every day, as long as you are awake, forever. The best thing to tell anybody is to remember to feel this. I have been doing this for a long time, and it is the best and most important feeling of all. I am very happy I could tell you this. Maybe someday we will meet face to face. Maybe. Anyway, at least you and I will always know that at least one other person somewhere is remembering and feeling and loving the Mystery right now.

About Da Free John

M aster Da Free John was born Franklin Albert Jones on November 3, 1939, in Jamaica, New York. The story of his early life, as told in his spiritual autobiography *The Knee of Listening*, involved the conscious sacrifice of the Illumined condition of "the Bright" that he knew at birth and the fulfillment of a unique ordeal of spiritual discipline and Awakening. At the age of thirty-one, he Awakened to perfect God-Realization and has devoted his entire life to serving the Divine Awakening of others.

Master Da Free John was born in the West, but he is neither a conventional Western man of religion and action nor a conventionally ascetic "swami" in the traditional style of Eastern adepts. Just so, the Way of Divine Grace, which he Teaches, is neither an inward or other-worldly Eastern religion nor a materialistic Western philosophy, oriented to the fulfillment of desires in this world. Rather, the Way that he Teaches is a unique communication of the living Truth, free of all binding cultural and philosophical influences, and thus accessible to all modern men and women. This Way reconciles and transcends the psycho-physical and cultural tensions of East and West, and it serves the renewal of a truly human, religious, and spiritual culture on Earth. This Radical Way is Taught and lived on the basis of the Wisdom of Perfect Enlightenment, as embodied in the Person of Da Free John.

An Invitation

If you would like to learn more about possible forms of involvement with the radical Teaching of Master Da Free John and the educational services of The Laughing Man Institute of The Johannine Daist Communion, please write:

The Laughing Man Institute
of The Johannine Daist Communion
750 Adrian Way
San Rafael, CA 94903